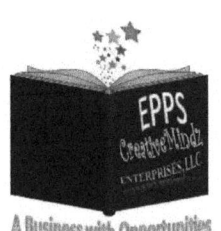

Copyright ©2016

Epps CreativeMindz Publishing

ISBN-10:0-9980567-2-3
ISBN-13:978-0-9980567-2-2

All rights reserved. No part of this publication may be reproduced, stored in a retrieval system, or transmitted, in any form, or by any means, electronic, mechanical, photocopying, recording, or otherwise, without the prior consent of the publisher.

Forward

Life takes one through many transitions and many phases. Sometimes those transitions can be the most elated feelings in the world, and other times it can feel like the lowest most devastating experience of life. What if you were told that both experiences, the highs and the lows were a necessity in life, to help make you a better, more equipped, more efficient and stronger version of yourself? Would you believe it, comprehend it, understand it?

If we only experienced the good in life how would we gain the wisdom from our trials, be inspired from our tribulations, and motivated from our failures to want, have, and do better in life? Jeremiah 29:11 says, "For I know the plans I have for you," declares the Lord, "plans to prosper you and not to harm you, plans to give you hope and a future." God knows that we will have obstacles in life, but he clearly states here that they were sent to develop us for our futures.

Life can throw us many curve balls, and sometimes situations that literally take our breath away, but the one thing that we have is the decision and the determination to say, "I will keep going!"

As you read this inspirational toolkit for your life, you will be motivated, inspired, and gain the wisdom that you need to help you face and maneuver through some of those tough issues of life. Life doesn't stop because difficulties happen. Life keeps going, and so should you. You were created to have life, and have it more abundantly (Ref. John 10:10). Don't be robbed of your inheritance.

Shanitria N. Kittrell
Best Selling Author
Motivational Speaker
Executive Coach

Keep Moving Forward

There is Only

One

Direction

"Keep Moving Forward"

Serenity Prayer

God, grant me the serenity

To accept the things, I cannot change,

Courage to change the things I can,

and wisdom to know the difference.

In Jesus Name Amen

God, give us grace to accept with serenity

the things that cannot be changed,

courage to change the things

which should be changed,

and the wisdom to distinguish

the one from the other.

Living one day at a time,

Enjoying one moment at a time,

Accepting hardship as a pathway to peace,

Taking, as Jesus did,

This sinful world as it is,

Not as I would have it,

Trusting that You will make all things right,

If I surrender to Your will,

So that I may be reasonably happy in this life,

And supremely happy with You forever in the next.

Amen.

"If you can't fly then run, if you can't run then walk, if you can't walk then crawl, but whatever you do you have to keep moving forward."

~ Dr. Martin Luther King Jr.

Be the Creator of your Destiny; Unveil your Purpose!

-Author DuWanda S. Epps

Don't Quit

When things go wrong as they sometimes will,

When the road you're on seem so far,

When the funds are low and the debts are high

you want to smile, but you have a frown,

When life is pressing you down a bit,

You seem lost or you don't have away.

Life is filled with twists and turns,

As we all know,

many a failure and mistakes

But life is a lesson, so learn from it;

Don't give up even when pace seems slow

You fall but get back up and keep moving,

Success comes when you keep working,

Don't hide when the silver tint clouds are near,

Your faith is being tested and you break through maybe near

So stand firm when things seem at its worst

Be victorious & courageous

Don't Quit!

~ Author DuWanda S. Epps

Happiness keeps you smile,

Trial keeps you strong,

Tears keep you human,

Failures keeps you determined

Success keep you humble

But God keeps you going!

Author DuWanda S. Epps

She is clothed in Strength & Dignity and she laughs

without fear of the Future

Proverbs 31:25

Faith is taking a first step even when you don't see

the whole staircase

Keep Moving Forward

Your pain has a purpose

Roman 5:3-5

The tallest oak in the forest was once just a little nut

that held its ground

To believe a thing is impossible is to make it so

If you want to grow, and you want to change, you must learn to let go of the habits and excuses that's keeping you in the past

You can't be who are going to be, and who you used to be at the same time.

-T D Jakes

I am convinced that life is 10% of what happened to you and 90% how you react to it.

The only thing that hurts harder than a failure is not

trying

-Apoorve Dubey

Limits are only the ones you set for yourself;

You got to Achieve

When you adopt a positive attitude

The key is to always look for the good in any given circumstance

Be ready

Stay Focus

Even through the Storms

Stay hungry & determined

Even when things seem cloudy

Keep You 're eyes on your prize

Be observant, be aware of your surrounding

Never give up

Keep going

Take pride in all you do

He who is not courageous enough to take risk will

accomplish nothing in life

-Muhammed Ali
(1942-2016)

You have 100% control over your response to events

in life

Live

Life

To

The

Fullest

Don't be can what you don't like

Doubt kills more dream than failure

Do the right thing,

in spite of what the other person is doing

"I am the greatest ever. I said that before I knew I was" - Muhammad Ali

Remember how are blessed you are.

Don't take anything for granted

Always be proud of who you see when you look in

the mirror

Always walk with your head held high

You can accomplish anything you put your mind too.

Never give up,

something take time;

So be patient and humble.

When a sister fall, her sister will always life her up

Through sisterhood sisters stick together.

Always read the fine,

there holds important information

Silent voices can't be heard

Pay attention to detail

Love yourself first before you can truly love another

If you pay with your life, others will too

Always be true to yourself.

If a person is not true to themselves don't expect them

to be true to you.

Worry about nothing and pray about everything.

Be a positive role model for others.

Leadership defines integrity and character

There is not such word as you can't

No is not final

Power Manifestation of the Universe

Like attracts like

Thoughts creates situations and circumstances:

You get what you think and speak about

You have the capability to bring forth what you want

in your life

Be cautious: Positive thoughts attract positive events

&

Negative thoughts attract negative events

If your feelings and thoughts consist of hardships and

obstacles, then hardship & obstacles will be what you

get

Embrace all the possibilities, keep thinking and expecting success without allowing doubts, you will eventually achieve what seemed impossible

It is not enough just to wish for something, you need strong desire and faith to manifest what you want.

In order for your thoughts to manifest, you have to repeat them often, and add feelings, desire and interest.

Your mind functions like a magnet

Similar energy attracts similar energy

Positive equals Positive

Negative equals Negative

Your thoughts are dormant they

determine the way you live

Law of Attraction is used daily, though mostly unconsciously

Stress kills, filling the mind with worries, toxicants

and anxieties brings stress, unhappiness & death

Filling your mind with happy thoughts and you will

attract happier days to come

Courage is like a muscle

We strengthen it with use

A woman is the full circle.

Within her there is power to create, nurture and the

ability to transform.

Love is what we were born with

Fear is what we have learned

No one can make you fear them,

without your consent

No need for a wishbone when you have a backbone

The most effective way of doing something,

is to just do it

The secret of getting ahead is getting started

Women are wiser than men because they know less

and understand more

Women have a wonderful instinct about things;

They can discover everything except the obvious

Break free from mental war fare

You can be your worst critic

Realize when the times and season are changing

If you have ever been broken,

you are still in the arms of God!

No matter what, people will talk

some are excited that you break free for the warfare.

Some are mad you made it out of the warfare

Never live so desperate that you cling to people that don't want any good for you

Not every place, people or thing is healthy for you

Be careful

You have to get beyond the loses in life

In order to gain happiness

With walls up

You will miss your opportunity

Walls are barriers

Barrier when you have experienced hurt and pain

In order to be victorious

Your barriers need to be destroyed

Sometimes there are lesson that must learned in

hardship

How you end is more important than how you begin

You are a choice away from a better life

Make it

Be mindful

Every choice comes with unchosen consequences

Good or Bad

It is possible to have good spiritual grounding and be

a wreck emotionally and physically

Our issues are sent by God to instruct us.

Just stay quiet

Sit back and watch the actions of ours

Self-Peace is the Key

Where there is hope there is Faith

Where there is faith Miracles happen

Attract what you expect

Reflect what you desire

Become what you respect

And Mirror what you admire

What Beauty looks like

Encouragement

Acceptance,

Forgivingness and

Compassion

Admire the individuals who choose to shine even

after all the storms they've been through

Don't be angry at all the people who told you No,

Instead thank them because of them you did it by

yourself

You cannot hang out with negative people

and

expect positive

Some people actual only check on you to see if you

failed yet!!

A Dream written down with a date becomes a goal.

A goal broken down into steps becomes a plan.

A plan backed by action makes your Dreams

A Plan in Action.

Checklist to Self

- ✓ Keep going
- ✓ Keep praying
- ✓ Stay positive
- ✓ Be determine
- ✓ Be Patient
- ✓ Become an Achiever

Never take someone's feelings for granted because

you never know how much courage that they took to

show it to you.

Don't look for love

Realize you are worth love looking for you

God all use your deepest pain

To be used as the greatest calling

You fall,

Rise Make mistake,

learn from them

Have confidence

Have faith

Continue putting one foot in front of the other

And continue to move forward

Confidence is beautiful

It does not matter the size, color, sex or age

Be confidence in who you are

And

Trust you are beautiful

Pray for guidance, strength when you feel lost,

confused or alone

He will clear your mind and direct your path

Just ask and believe.

Prayer and Faith

Be thankful for God not giving up on you when you

gave up on yourself

The hardest things in the World is the say "I am

Sorry"

And "I forgive you"

Be careful not to bring baggage to any relationship

Baggage only weights you down

Release it

And set yourself free

Faith does not rest in the wisdom of men,

But in the power of God.

1 Corinthians 2:5

Placed in places for a reason, meeting the right people

longer than a season.

God can bring peace to your past

Purpose to your present and hope to your future

John 14:27

You're going into a season where you're about to

experience

Breakthrough after breakthrough because what you

went through didn't break you

God is within her she will not fall

Psalm 45:6

Every day is a blessing

Rejoice and be glad in it

Rise Up

Get a fresh start

Engage in bright opportunities

Each and Everyday

There is no love without forgiveness

And there is no forgiveness without love

Forgiveness is the key to your freedom

There is nothing wrong

with owning up to something when you did wrong

Its shows courage

In life you have to go through the worst, just to get to

the best

Women were created differently because men can't

adore our pain.

A woman will look like she wasn't crying the night

before

She believed and so she did

I've been knocked down put down and let down so I

know when my sister falls to lift her up

When the road gets though, don't be afraid just

change your shoes

Why play with fire, when all you have to do is put it

out.

When you do an assessment on individuals around you and if you have a X by their name that affirmation they need to go. X means exit

Discover you own inner strength and take your

power back and make a transformation.

Reaching your goals does not bring happiness, but

the journey you took to get there.

In the mist of pain, later had something worth writing

about.

Silence creates a self-made bomb waiting to explode.

With my growth came wisdom and with wisdom

come understanding

Your situation does not determine your final

destination

I had made many mistakes to the perfect but I have

too many blessing to be ungrateful.

Success prompts determination and hard work

Success don't embrace laziness or procrastination.

When the Lord speaks listen attentively

If he trying to get you attention, trust he will gain it another way.

Creative minds don't sleep

Business minded people brain is always working

Art is all shapes and colors joining together

Creativity defines artistic minds and hands at work.

When you find strength from God you remain

faithful and loyal no matter what loss or pain you had

felt.

Pain can promote positive change

#Roc'On#UrWorthy#

It's starts with you!

When you receive 1. No, 2. No and even 3. No...

don't give up..

Be humble, Patient and Determine...

The Yes/ Door(s) is about to OPEN!...

Be the Creator of your Destiny; Unveil your Purpose!

-Author DuWanda S. Epps

Sometimes in the mist of pain, it rains to wash away

the pain.

Pain brings about positive change

Pain create preparation for what's to come in the

future.

Life is designed to be unseen but the Lord grants us

with serenity.

Gods plan isn't our own.

Women were created differently because men can't

adore our pain.

A woman will look like she wasn't crying the night

before

She believed and so she did

A woman possesses a lot of power she just let some

people borrow it

Blessed, determined, hungry and humble

It doesn't make sense now but soon you will know.

Stand firm, be determined and patient humble and blessed.

Another day is a blessings providing opportunity to change tomorrow

When God has an assignment on your life, you must complete it!

Treat others the like you want to be treated

A married man or woman

Should be off limits

Have faith small as a mustard seed

Prayer answer things

You can teach a person of know it all already

They are not willing to learn

Times is of the essences

Once it's gone you

Won't get it back

No such thing as catching up on sleep

One hour lost will take 2 days to gain back

Be true to yourself

Leopards don't change their spots

Practice safe sex

Saves life's

Have standards

saves a lot of headaches

Only if you allow it

It will happen and/or continue

Your body should be your temple

Treat it as such

Learn to listen to your body

It speaks truth

Every day will not be the same

Be your children's first role model

Have morals and values

Tears is not a show of fear

Be thankful

For life

Whether the storm

Sunshine will come

Time heals old wounds

Because you were hurt in the past

Don't allow that to define your future

Be responsible

Be accountable

For your actions

Trust your gut

Be Bold

Creative

Courageous

Be Beautiful

Attitude can make you or break you

You are capable to change

Don't depend on others to put a smile on your face!

Good vibes only

Hastag #UrWorthy#Roc'On

You got to believe

Make it a habit. See every problem as an opportunity. As you regularly start to look for opportunities in a problem, as you continue to think of finding opportunities you will begin to attract more opportunities.

Steadfast- devoted, loyal to a person & belief

Be all you can be!

Don't let someone become a priority in your life…

When you are just an option in theirs

Situations can **MAKE** you or **BREAK** you!

Forgiveness meads broken wings

Remember broken wings can't fly

Three Self-Motivational Competencies:

Achievement Drive: Striving to improve or meet a standard of excellence.

Commitment: Embracing the organization's or groups vision and goals.

Initiative and Optimism: Encourage people to seize opportunities and allow them to take setbacks and obstacles in stride.

When the smoke clears

See Who is still standing

Praise him

Because

He is Worthy

Give him your

Highest

Praise

Who are you?

Look in the mirror ask yourself

People watch and report how you go through your

dark moments

Don't judge a book by its cover

Clarify the story

Before you believe all

you are told

Be careful not to attract

People just like you

Watch how you model yourself!

Men know how to approach a woman

It determines how she carry yourself

#FACTS#

Listen to Our Elders

Value

Respect

Appreciate

Them all because if it was not for them

We would not be but where we are

Because they

LABORED FOR US TODAY

You need to connect with the right people

When you're down

When you get to the top

Reach down and pull someone up

Don't be selfish

You can't just be satisfied

You have to CONTINUE striding

Change your way of thinking

Change IF to When

Claim it

Don't just settle for a little

God will bless you with a lot

Don't careful how you treat people

Push until something happen

"Develop an attitude of gratitude, and give thanks for everything that happens to you, knowing that every step forward is a step toward achieving something bigger and better than your current situation."

~ Brian Tracy

The power has and always will be within you, but nothing will happen until you get and stay motivated to make something happen, to change your life and achieve your desires. Self-motivation empowers you and helps you keep your spirit high no matter how discouraging a situation is.

Get rid of negative emotions

Your attitude can change things

For the better or worse

Shift your focus

Don't focus on the problems, focus on finding opportunities. Don't talk about a problem; talk about an opportunity. When you see a problem as a problem you only attract more problems. If you wish to attract opportunities instead, see the problem as an opportunity. There is an old saying that goes like this: "There are no problems, only opportunities."

Set backs are only the opportunity to for a fresh good

Read between the lines

Sometimes you need to look through different lens

Take others perspective into consideration

Allow various views to present opportunities.

The brain is like a sponge

Absorb positivity

What may seem to be a failure can actually lead to

new opportunities

Your "I can do it" attitude

Is your successor

To unlocking your future

Seize each opportunity

The worse thing to do is miss it

Or

Mess it up

Capture your moments

You hold the power to overcome

Any situation

When you treat your problems

Like problems

You create more problems

Food for thought

When you treat your opportunities

Like opportunities

You create more opportunities

Random thoughts are the most creative ones

Unveil your creativity within

When you're at the top

Reach down grab others hand

Can't stop, Won't Stop

Keep on Push

Keep on Striving

Choose to be someone GREAT

The process of healing is to experience pain, then recognition and finally release

Steadfast with your **DREAM**

Always believe that something

Wonderful is about to happen regardless of the situation

There is light at the end of the tunnel

BELIEVE IT!!

Imagine with all your mind
Believe with all your heart
Achieve with all your might

International Selling Author DuWanda S. Epps

Owner of CreativeMindz Book Lounge in NC, three time Best Selling Author, International Selling, Publisher, Inspirational Speaker, Therapeutic Mentor, Co-Author of 5, Author of 15 books. Featured Guest on The Hotness #1 Online Radio Show- P.O.E.T. (People of Extraordinary Talent) in Alabama. July's Edition Cover Girl of Richmond hottest magazine.

Author DuWanda S. Epps, Graduated of Metropolitan College of New York earned degrees in Human Service, Public Administration. Currently in Graduate program to obtain Doctoral Degree in Public Administration at Capella University.

Founder of (EEL) Roc'On Collaborating with fellow Author and Founder of Ur Worthy Movement: Joining together to educate, empower and prevent DV and SA against women and men. Taking courage, strength and faith to take a Stand.

Non for Profit Cultivating Change II, Inc. (2010) assisting families in the community in need of clothing, food, household items and providing resources in the community for additional services and assistance.

- 3-year recipient of 2014-2015, 2015-2016, 2016-2017 One Warm Coat.
- 2015 receiver of a letter from Wesley Shelter, Director Mrs. White, Wilson, NC
- 3 year Adopt a family for Christmas.
- 15-year List of other asset to the community in the Eastern Carolinas and New York contributions.

Launched of Epps CreativeMindz Enterprise this past Spring 2016. Services include providing reasonable services for small businesses, authors, entertainers and all others with effective marketing and publishing services for their business or brand.

One of the brave women have opened up about their past hurt. Another enlighten, encourage and empowering reading for both men and women globally to show the world that we have turned our pain into #PASSION and #PURPOSE!

EEL Movement: Enchained (held Captive) *Exculpate (verb Forgive) *Liberate (Freedom).

With compassion to empower, embrace and strengthen women & families for 15 plus years. I am presently a project fund for Women Rebuilding & Transforming to provide 6-12 months of Life Coaching Services FREE to women rebuilding & transitioning in life and/or from battered shelters. My goal is to provide resilient empowerment and supportive outreach to promote self-sufficiency. http://www.plumfund.com/crowdfunding/eel-movement-sister-2-sister

Calling on other Authors who supports taking a stand for DV and SA. To assist our Empowering Library authors must donate (1) book per participating shelter with envisioning recognition in their name.

Working on Upcoming Projects & Opportunities includes these Anthologies:
1. Redefining Sisterhood (2017)

2. Daily Inspirational Devotion (2017)
3. Single Fathers Journey, I have a Heart.

New Released:
Broken Silence: Life After the Rain (Autobiography of DuWanda S. Conway)
Unleashed Em' Shackles been Broken (Self-help, Motivation, Encouragement)
Rhymes & Reasons
Naturally Beautiful Me
Sine me Libri Gloria
Naturellement Belle Me Activity
When I grow up
Als ich erwachsen warden

Soon Releases:
Women on a Mission
Fear to Freedom

Released:
Tre'Zure Box (erotica)
Flowin Emotions
Flowin Emotions ll (Self-help books)
Emociones Flowin II: Flowin Emotions ll
Pain 2 Passion: Our Valley Experience
Chocolate & Diamonds: Celebrating the Majesty of Motherhood

Children Selections:
Friends & Me

Amis et moi
Amigos y Me
Hooray 4 Learning (English & Spanish Learning)

Just Filmed- Short Film/ Documentary:
A short film about an African American woman's story of triumph, abuse, and faith. The main character witnesses' domestic violence as a child, then grows up to be in a violent relationship herself. She also experiences sexual abuse as well as being a homeless pregnant teen. Her broken marriage leads to a near drug overdose. Despite the hurt and pain, she is able to graduate high school, college and earn a Master's Degree at the age of 25. A world of struggles did not keep her from being the woman and living the life destined for her.

Stay Tune Broken Silence: Life After the Rain
Stage Play 2017

Stay Connected:

www.flowinemotions.weebly.com
www.authordsepps.com
https://www.linkedin.com/in/authordsepps
authordsepps@outlook.com
Twitter: **flowinemotions**
Instagram: **BestSellinAuthorDSE**
www.eppscreativemindzenterprise.com
www.creativemindzbooklounge.com

www.ingramcontent.com/pod-product-compliance
Lightning Source LLC
Chambersburg PA
CBHW051839090426
42736CB00011B/1874